On the Nature and Dignity of Love

D1320151

THE COLUMBA SERIES

William of Saint Thierry

On the Nature and Dignity of Love

Translated from the Latin by
GEOFFREY WEBB AND ADRIAN WALKER

London
The Saint Austin Press
MMI

Nihil Obstat: CAROLUS DAVIS, S.T.L.
Imprimatur: E. MORROGH BERNARD, *Vic. Gen.*
Westmonasterii, die 8a Decembris, 1954

The Saint Austin Press
296 Brockley Road
London
SE4 2RA
Tel +44 (0)20 8692 6009
Fax +44 (0)20 8469 3609
Email: books@saintaustin.org
Website: www.saintaustin.org

ISBN 1901157 54 7
First published by Mowbrays in 1956

Design and typography of this edition © The Saint Austin Press, 2001.

Printed by Newton Design & Print Ltd, London, UK.   www.newtondp.co.uk

INTRODUCTION

WILLIAM OF SAINT THIERRY, the little known but very great contemporary and friend of Saint Bernard, wrote his treatise *On the nature and dignity of love* a little after his first work, *On contemplating God*. He was at the time abbot of the Benedictine monastery of Saint Thierry near Rheims, but one already notices how heavy he found the abbatial charge. Eventually he found it impossible to carry on any longer, and in 1135 he resigned his office and took the Cistercian habit in the new foundation at Signy.

Most of William's work was produced when he was abbot of Saint Thierry, and his treatise *On the nature and dignity of love* might conceivably be based on sermons delivered at the morning chapter to his monks at Saint Thierry.

As Saint Aelred took Cicero's doctrine as the basis for his work on spiritual friendship, so the author of *The nature and dignity of love* took Ovid's *Art of Loving* as the starting point of his work. But whereas Aelred developed Cicero's thought in a Christian context, William used Ovid only in order to contradict his all too popular doctrine of profane love, as he says quite clearly in his first chapter: '. . . by unruly rules he [Ovid] instructed the natural faculties in licentiousness . . . instead of turning towards God in the due order of nature, men were brought low by the allurements of the flesh.' One can legitimately suppose that William found many of the novices as saturated with Ovid as he found them in later years at Signy reeking with the 'errors' of Abelard.

William visualized the monastery as a school of love.

In chapter nine we read that 'the monastery is charity's own school. Here the study of love is pursued. Here love's disputations are held and love's questions answered.' But it is important to note how, in the same chapter, William traces the descent of the monastic community from that fellowship of the Holy Spirit which the Apostles were the first to enjoy. *On the nature and dignity of love* is not just a monastic idyll, but a message which must interest every Christian, for all are bound to seek after the perfection of love.

Love begins as a neutral faculty of doing good or evil indifferently. The direction taken by desire is specified either by self-will which inclines to sin, or by the coming of the Holy Spirit (Who is the will of the Father and the Son) Who turns the human will into love. Chapter seven gives a complete analysis of the human faculty of loving— a favourite Cistercian subject, dwelt on at length by Aelred and Bernard too. As the loves of man are rearranged under the influence of grace into their original hierarchy, so the image of God in the soul regains more and more of its original beauty. The highest form of love is charity, by means of which the soul cleaves inseparably to God, forming all its judgements by the light of His countenance, and ordering all its actions according to the holy will of God, which is learned inwardly, as we read in chapter seven. Higher even than charity William places wisdom, *sapientia*, which is of an intellectual rather than of an affective significance. It is equivalent to knowing and tasting truth as God Himself knows and tastes it. It is to follow the truth of God's own mind, now made one's own way of thinking and understanding. This, too, is the result of the Holy Spirit's working in the soul, for is He not the wisdom of the Trinity, in the same way that He is its love?

A note should perhaps be added about a much discussed

passage in this work. It begins in the final paragraph of chapter four, and continues in chapter five, where William insists that the saint is stable in righteousness. He holds strongly that although a man may obey the law of the flesh and of sin, love remains intact if he does so against his will. This is because the seed of his spiritual rebirth protects him from within: elsewhere William expresses this inward protection more clearly, and says that it is due to the grace of God and the indwelling of the Holy Spirit.

We can say that, for the holy man, sin, although still theoretically possible, is a practical impossibility and highly improbable. Or we can give a second and more detailed explanation. It seems that William allows of sin, but he maintains that in the holy soul love remains constant and the stable disposition of the soul is undisturbed. Arguing from Saint John's words, 'whosoever is born of God committeth not sin, for His seed abideth in him, and he cannot sin because he is born of God,' he states that perfect charity, being a stable thing, persists even in sin: so much so that Saint Peter did not lose charity when he sinned.

Saint Thomas Aquinas quotes this passage[1] and rejects it, for he says that one mortal sin brings about a loss of charity, since any grave sin is completely inconsistent with it. This is because, for Saint Thomas, charity is an 'infused virtue'; it necessarily has a supernatural and divine character, and it cannot exist in the presence of any serious sin at all.

But, for William, charity is the strong habit of love which is embedded in thought and will. It has become second nature to the perfect soul, and that fundamental disposition can never be disturbed, whatever may happen on the surface. The soul will turn back to God with all the energy of its love if it is temporarily deflected from Him. There is always this conflict of flesh and spirit in which the flesh seems to be an alien principle, but in spite of it, the love of God does not fail. As he expresses it in his ninth meditation, 'my spirit always loved Thee, even when my flesh neglected Thee.'[2] For when forces which do not belong to the soul's true self turn it from its object, we may say even then that the soul is loving God and striving to attain Him.

The text used for the translation is that of Migne, *P.L.*, Vol. 184, and Mlle Davy's new edition with French translation (Bibliothèque des Textes Philosophiques, Vrin, 1953) has been consulted wherever the Migne text seemed doubtful. Scriptural quotations have been taken from various versions and references are to the Vulgate. For permission to quote from Mgr. Knox's translation of the Bible, we have to thank the publishers, Messrs. Burns, Oates & Washbourne.

G. W.
A. W.

CONTENTS

ON THE NATURE AND DIGNITY
OF LOVE

CHAPTER I

THE ART OF LOVE

THE art of all arts is the art of loving, and the teaching of
this art belongs exclusively to God. But since God has
rooted love in our very nature, it is equally true to say
that nature is our teacher. And when love, which is of free
and noble birth, preserves its liberty in the face of deceiving
passions, we may count love itself as the third professor
of this art. The pupil for his part must be willing to learn
what love has to teach, and he must be obedient to God.

Love is a power which carries the soul along by a natural
tendency towards its destination. Every creature, whether
spiritual or physical, has a place which God has designed
for it, and a tendency which moves it in the right direction.
Philosophy tells us that this tendency is not always a weight
in the strict sense, dragging a thing downwards. Water goes
down, it is true, but fire goes up. Man for his part has a
natural bent by which his spirit tends towards higher things
and his body to the things of the earth; but in both cases
the direction is towards a natural destination or goal.
Of the body's destination we read, 'Dust thou art, and unto
dust thou shalt return,'[3] and the Book of Wisdom tells us
that 'the spirit will return to God Who gave it.'[4] If you
observe a corrupt man you will see how his tendencies
are carrying him to his end. But when all goes according

to God's plan, the spirit returns to its Maker and the body is put back into the earth where it is resolved into the elements, from which it was originally formed. When earth, air, fire, and water reclaim the bodily particles which are theirs, and the bond which held them all together comes to break, then each particle returns by its natural tendency to the element from which it came. And it is left to each one of us to say whether we prefer to think of this process as corruption, or merely as the natural resolution of the body into its original elements.

While it is impossible for any of these particles to wander from the path mapped out for it by nature, the poor soul, despite its natural bent towards God, does not know how to return to its origin. Or at least it only learns with difficulty, since it is corrupted by sin. It is always turning in the direction of its origin since it longs for happiness. It dreams of happiness, and seeks for nothing else. 'Happy is he, and none other, whose God is the Lord.'[5] But in seeking happiness where it is not to be found, and by means which cannot lead to it, man wanders far from the goal towards which he is directed, and which it is natural for him to seek by loving. And so, having neglected nature's teaching, he must needs have a man to instruct him in the search for happiness, and to tell him where and how, in what place and by what paths he must seek.

Love, as we have said, is naturally rooted in the human soul by the Author of nature. But after the law of God has been put aside, love must be taught by a man. It must not be taught as if it were something which no longer existed in the soul, but rather the soul must learn how to purify the love which it already has. Once upon a time, the corrupt love of the flesh had its masters, and they were so skilled in their subject that the most famous of them was constrained, even by the lovers and companions of his depravity, to recant by praising the opposite of what he had originally preached. After he had written an incitement to carnal love, he was forced to write about its cure.[6] He had racked his brains to invent new contrivances to arouse sensual desire, and had related detestable stories of the past. By unruly rules he instructed the natural faculties in licentiousness. By unnecessary incitements to lewdness he urged them on to madness, and in this way the natural order in men perished. Instead of turning towards God in the due order of nature, men were brought low by the allurements of the flesh. Their souls, understanding nothing, were 'compared to senseless beasts and became like to them.'[7] God could have said of them, 'My Spirit shall not remain in man because he is flesh,'[8] and they for their part could have said, 'My heart is become like wax, melting in the midst of my bowels.'[9] For the heart, being placed more or less in the narrow central part of the body, between the higher and the lower senses, governs the body together with all the surrounding territory of the thoughts and actions, like a king in his realm. But when heated by fleshly desires, it melts into a degenerate softness and flows down into the belly; that is to say, it has a taste only for the things of the belly. From the belly it sinks even lower, defiling and perverting the natural feeling of love into brutish lusts. These men not only desire the unlawful abuse of the body by shameful passions. They are so forgetful of their former excellence, that man, who was created for God alone, is regarded by those who have corrupted him and those he has seduced, as the natural dwelling place of excesses and the den of all vice. He is the really unhappy man, who, despite nature's protests, has become sufficiently foul in his own eyes to turn his soul into a palace for Satan, when by right it belongs to God the Creator, and to Him alone.

CHAPTER II

THE ORIGIN OF LOVE

LET us begin our treatise at the place where love itself begins, and follow its progress through the passing years right up to its old age, which, instead of being full of sorrow and sickness, is a time when God's mercy abounds more than ever. Just as with the passing of time a child grows into a youth, and the youth becomes a man and grows old, his changing characteristics providing him with three changes of name, so it is, too, with the growth of virtue. The will grows into love, love becomes charity, and charity develops into wisdom. When speaking of love, we must not forget to make mention of the place of its birth and the nobility of its lineage. Its birthplace is God; there it is born, and nursed, and there it grows up. There it is a citizen, a native, and no foreigner. Love is the gift of God alone and it remains in Him. Love is due to God only, and for no other reason than God Himself. We must add that God, Who is one in three persons, created man in His own image, imprinting in him a certain likeness to the Trinity, in which God's image was to shine. This likeness was given to the new dweller on earth so that he might cleave to his Creator of his own free will, in the way that like things are always attracted by their like. For if this lesser, created trinity did not cleave to its Maker, it would be lured and seduced by the many different kinds of creatures, and would wander away from the Trinity Which made it.

When the Trinity created man by breathing into his

face the breath of life (that is to say, his spiritual and mental powers, and the powers of life, growth and movement), God placed in his head the faculty of memory, so that he might always remember the goodness and power of his Creator. Then, without any interval of time, memory generated reason, and from memory and reason proceeded the will. Thus the memory possesses and contains in itself the term to which man should tend. The reason knows that he should so tend, and the will actually tends towards the term. These three faculties are a unity, although they are three efficient powers. In the divine Trinity there is one substance but Three Persons. God the Father generates God the Son, and God the Holy Spirit proceeds from Them both. Likewise memory generates reason, and from these two proceeds the will. Now in order that the rational soul created in man may cleave strongly to God, the Father claims the memory for His own, and Son takes the reason for Himself, and the Holy Spirit Who proceeds from Them both, claims the will (which springs from memory and reason).

At its birth, then, love is nothing other than the will. We have seen its cradle, its birth and the manner of its adoption, its dignity and nobility. The will, under the influence of grace with which it now co-operates, cleaves and consents to the Holy Spirit, Who is the Love and the Will of Father and Son. It begins to desire ardently just those things which God wants for it, and which reason and memory show to be desirable. And through this strong desire, the will becomes love, for love is nothing but a determined orientation of the will towards a good. In itself the will is simply a disposition rooted in the rational soul, capable of doing both good and evil indifferently. It does good with the help of grace, but when left to its own devices it does evil. In order that the human soul may be complete and lacking in nothing, God makes the will entirely free. From this it follows that the will may chose either alternative. If it co-operates with grace it becomes, and is called, virtue, or love, as we have already said. If, on the other hand, the will should wish to enjoy nothing but itself, it immediately proves its own weakness and is called by as many different names as it has vices, such as avarice, cupidity, sensuality, and so on.

The will in its freedom is set at the junction of two ways, like the Pythagorean symbol of the two-branched letter 'Y'. If it rises up to that dignity which is proper to it by reason of the powers with which God originally endowed it, and turns into love, it will then proceed (in virtue of the natural unfolding of these powers) to develop from love into charity. And this charity will come to its full perfection in the form of wisdom. But if this order is broken, God in His justice will allow the will to be dragged down to its ruin, covered in darkness and buried in the pit of vice, unless grace comes quickly to its aid. Only then can the will leave the road to hell and begin to direct its steps to higher things. If it follows the grace which helps and nourishes it, it will grow up into love. It starts off filled with the courage that goes with extreme youth, and from the spirit of fear which makes it dread punishment, it advances towards the spirit of piety, in which it will taste new graces. Thus it will begin to love God faithfully and adore Him, for it is written: 'Piety is the worship of God.'[10] Let this youthful love only show the strength which goes not so much with years as with goodness. Let it not lose the enthusiasm of youth, nor on the other hand let it allow this to deviate from its natural use. If those who have the souls of beasts and the flesh of asses, as the prophet says,[11] are driven to madness by the passing things which seduce them, much more can those who are possessed of true love and surrendered to its leading, abandon themselves as they will to the passions of spiritual youth. Is it not a sad thing indeed, if those who corrupt nature are more successful in doing evil, than the lovers of truth are in doing good?

Listen to these words of madness: 'If we were out of our mind it was for God. If we are sane it is for you.'[12] And again, 'Either forgive them this trespass, or if Thou do not, strike me out of the book that Thou hast written.'[13] 'For I could wish to be anathema from Christ, for the sake of my brethren.'[14] However holy his motive may seem, does not the apostle give you the impression that he is mad? For he is firmly resolved to desire that which is in fact impossible—to be anathema from Christ for Christ's sake. Such was the drunkenness of the apostles when the Holy Spirit came upon them. Such was the reason for Festus saying to Paul: 'Paul, thou art mad.'[15] Is it surprising if he was called mad who, even at the point of death, strove to convert to Christ those men by whom he was judged for the sake of Christ? It was not his great learning that brought this madness on him, as the king claimed who knew the true reason, but pretended he did not. But as we have said, it was because he was drunk with the Holy Spirit that he longed to make those who judged him like himself. What madness could be greater, or more surprising, than that of a man who has left the world behind because of his yearning for Christ, yet cleaves to the world for Christ's sake; that is, under the compulsion of obedience and brotherly love? He strives after heaven, and yet sinks himself in the mire. Like the youth Benjamin in the psalm he is completely carried away.[16] Such was the madness which made the martyrs laugh in the midst of their torments. I might even use that phrase of Virgil, 'it is good to be mad.'[17]

CHAPTER III

THE PROGRESS OF LOVE

AT this stage it is fitting that youthful ardour should take the upper hand, so that the paths of religion may be more swiftly run. Neither should passion be in any way restrained, for the reason is bridle enough. It is not right for a beginner to be indulgent towards himself, although he must be indulgent towards others. He must judge himself with severity, but he must be gently and obediently humble towards the fathers and brothers who guide and counsel him. If the right kind of severity and the right kind of indulgence are lacking in him, or if he loses heart, I do not hope for his perseverance in the path of religious life. But if he fails to persevere, then I fear his destruction. A beginner's whole desire should be to make himself foolish in all things for Christ's sake, and to depend on the will of others, especially if he has an older man whose teaching he may trust as having been learnt from God before it was preached to men. Here again, he who is a beginner in obedience must not grant himself freedom of judgement, unless, of course, anything is commanded which is manifestly against God's will. Freedom of judgement can only come after long experience and patience have given his mind full understanding in these matters. But he should try especially to practice that obedience of which it is written: 'Purifying your souls in the obedience of charity.'[18] For this is the will of God, pleasing and perfect.

The constant help of careful and enduring prayer must

be sought, in order to win these things and to keep them. Faith in prayer must be great enough to hope for all things. Devotion must be strong enough to seem to force God's hand. Love must be so intense as to feel that it receives in prayer all that it seeks. Humility must show so good a will as to desire above all things that God's will, not its own, be done in everything. The beginner in obedience must embrace cleanness of heart, purity of body, and silence, or well controlled speech. His eyes must not wander. He must not look proud. His ears must not be itching to hear. If he is temperate in food and sleep, he will not hinder the efficacy of a diet of good works. His hands should be held in check and his gait should be quiet. Lewdness of heart should not burst out in a loud laugh, but a sweet smile should show its grace. He must be conscientious in reading and meditation—and these should be spiritual and not prompted by mere curiosity. He must show subjection to his superiors; he must reverence the elder brethren and cherish the younger ones. He must not wish to be in a position of authority, but must love to be commanded. He must wish to be useful to everyone. He must not let severity overwhelm him, nor mildness make him soft. Let him have cheerfulness in his face and sweetness in his heart towards all, and kindness in all his acts. For this is the time and place for sloughing off sensuality, for rooting out vice and breaking self-will. When his former desires have been pruned away like useless twigs, the desires of his true nature will have greater hope of being fulfilled. For his former inclinations were not true desires but rather lusts: 'the lust of the flesh, the lust of the eyes and the pride of life.'[19]

And now, let him who loves the more run the faster. This is where we find toil and drudgery because love is still blind, and does what it does without knowing whither it is going or whence it comes. Love uses its feelings as a blind man uses his hands. If he is doing something with his hands, he can see neither the thing he is making nor his hands which make it. And just as a man with normal sight might instruct a blind man in some work or other by bending him, straightening him up, moving and exercising him in what looks more like a mechanical action than a craft; so too, by all the means mentioned in the previous chapter, blind love is formed exteriorly in a certain integrity of life and behaviour. But when the substance of the inner man has been softened up by the long practice of penance, and has been thereby impressed and informed anew, he will produce the pleasant fruits of salvation. Then in deed and not merely in appearance will he understand the usefulness of these and similar observances.

At this moment, however, observance is not yet loved, but only willed, since commanded by the reason. As I said of the blind man, although his eyes cannot see, his hands do not cease to work. Likewise, he who wishes to become perfect in great things must be faithful in the very least, and he sings to God in the words of the psalm: 'I am consumed with longing for thine ordinances.'[20] Let him then show his good intention in that over which, by God's bounty, he has power; I mean his body. Let him do what the Apostle says, 'Yield your members as slaves of justice unto sanctification, as once you yielded them as slaves of uncleanness unto iniquity.'[21] This is as if he said: 'When love has changed into charity, and the soul has reached its perfect purity, I will tell you something very different, something divine. I will no longer speak in a human way, as once I did, because of the weakness of your flesh. But for the present, take this merely human word.' And indeed, if a man is faithful in giving himself as a slave of justice unto sanctification, he will begin to feel as David did when he said: 'In

Thy Name I will lift up my hands. Let my soul be filled as with marrow and fatness.'[22] For if he mortifies the movements of the flesh by the spirit, and if he glorifies God in his actions, his soul will certainly be filled with the marrow of grace and the fatness of the Holy Spirit. He will begin to be made new 'in the spirit of his mind, and to put on the new man made in the image of God in justice and holiness of truth.'[23]

Then things take on a new appearance for him. The wonderful gifts of grace after which he has laboured begin to reveal themselves to him more familiarly. The body, for instance, which has been brought low by holy penance, submits itself by good habit and of its own accord to the mastery of the spirit. The interior countenance of man is renewed day by day, and his eyes are opened even to the point of gazing on the good things of God. Now sudden and frequent manifestations of God and of the saints in their shining begin to revive and light up the soul by the ceaseless desire they kindle. For wisdom, as Job says, 'going joyfully along the streets, hideth the light in his hands and commandeth it to come again. He showeth his friends concerning it, that it is his possession, and that he may come up to it.'[24]

Now the soul which has striven for so long, has on occasions a sweet and unwonted feeling in which she rests softly. She is grieved when it goes away and does not return at her plea. Like someone brought up in the country and used only to country fare, the first taste of these delights is for her like entering a king's court for the first time. When she is chased away it is hard for her to go back to her own poor home. She comes back again and again to the king's door, begging to be given something whenever the door opens, and at last she finds her way in. She runs headlong to the innermost room where Wisdom sits at table, and although she is sure to be turned out again, she sits down with the guests and hears the words: 'Eat your fill, my friends, and drink deep, my beloved.'[25]

Then there is born in her a love of holy poverty and the desire to be hidden; the dislike of worldly distractions, and the habit of prayer and psalmody.

CHAPTER IV

THE PRAISES OF TRUE CHARITY

But now a serious temptation comes out to meet the soul, and many there are whose progress it hinders. So far they have made good progress, but now they slow down, lose heart, and perhaps even turn back. The grace which was given them by their good Father to prevent them from fainting along the road, they begin to regard as a sufficient good in itself, or they take grace lightly and build up a false self-confidence. They boast either in their heart or in their words that God will never abandon them, whereupon their progress comes to a halt. They 'eat and drink judgement to themselves'[26] as often as they receive consolations from God, since they correspond to such favours by doing their own will and not the will of God. 'The enemies of the Lord,' the psalmist says, 'have lied to him and their punishment shall last for ever; and he fed them with the best of wheat and honey out of the rock.'[27] They are fed, but yet they are enemies; they are filled, but still they are liars. Notice that it is not only wheat, but the best of wheat; not the rock, but honey from the rock which they are given. This means that they have been filled with the hidden and divine grace of God's holy visitation, yet they are branded as enemies. If they had not been enemies they could not have been so quickly filled. He who is satisfied does not seek for more than he has received, because he is satisfied; what he has is enough for him. As the Apostle says: 'For those who were once enlightened, who have both tasted the heavenly gift and become partakers of the Holy

Spirit: who have tasted the good word of God and the powers of the world to come . . .'[28] for these, a deliberate sin committed after receiving knowledge of the truth, is a second crucifixion of the Son of God. They are treading underfoot the blood of the covenant through which they were sanctified, as if it were unclean. They are insulting the Spirit of grace. And to do evil that good may come of it, to sin boldly, presuming upon the merits of the Crucified—what is this but to crucify the Son of God all over again? If they would but hear what follows! 'The earth that drinks in the rain that often falls upon it, and produces vegetation that is of use to those by whom it is tilled, receives a blessing from God. But that which brings forth thorns and thistles is worthless, and is nigh unto a curse and its end is to be burnt.'[29] But enough of this. Let us return to better things—to those more perfect things which, as the Apostle says, are nearer to salvation.[30]

He who is not turned back at this point by temptation may be said to grow from youth into manhood, that is to say, into the age of the fulness of Christ. And now love begins to be strengthened, enlightened, and made constant, taking on the name of a more perfect virtue and of a higher dignity. This enlightened love is charity; a love from God, in God, and for God. Charity is God, and 'God is charity.'[31] A short praise for charity, but it sums up everything. Whatever can be said of God can also be said of charity. Considered according to the nature of gift and giver, the name of the substance of charity is in the giver, and the name of the quality of charity is in the gift. But we can call even the gift of charity 'God,' because above all the virtues, the virtue of charity cleaves to God and resembles Him.

What, indeed, shall we say of charity? We have heard report of it, but we have not known it or seen it. The

Apostle knew it and called it 'A yet more excellent way.' He spent himself completely in its praise, saying 'I point out to you a yet more excellent way. If I should speak with the tongues of men and angels but do not have charity, I have become as sounding brass or a tinkling cymbal. And if I have prophecy and know all mysteries and all knowledge, and if I have all faith so as to remove mountains, yet do not have charity, I am nothing. And if I distribute all my goods to feed the poor, and if I deliver my body to be burned, yet do not have charity, it profits me nothing. Charity is patient, is kind; charity does not envy, is not pretentious, is not puffed up, is not ambitious, is not self-seeking, is not provoked. It thinks no evil and does not rejoice over wickedness, but rejoices with the truth. Charity bears with all things, believes all things, hopes all things, endures all things. Charity never fails, whereas prophecies will disappear, and tongues will cease and knowledge will be destroyed. So there abide faith, hope and charity, these three. But the greatest of these is charity.'[32]

This is the sweet yoke of the Lord; the burden which carries and supports him who carries it. This is the light burden of the Gospels which is sweet to those to whom the Lord says: 'Now I do not call you servants but friends.'[33] To him who before could not bear the commandments of the law, the precepts of the Gospels are light through the assistance of grace. He who before could not obey the command 'thou shalt not kill,'[34] now finds it easy to lay down his life for the brethren. If too heavy a load is placed on a mule it will refuse to carry it, but if a light cart (by which we signify the Gospel which 'runs through the whole world'[35]) is brought, the animal will draw double the weight which it first refused, without any effort. A fledgling bird cannot support itself in the air, but when its wings and feathers grow it can fly without effort, even though these are an added weight. Yet another analogy can be taken from bread, which cannot be swallowed when it is very stale, but will go down easily if soaked in milk.

Love begins as an effort, with but little feeling in the soul. Charity is love's realization. The hand of charity works more easily when it has the help of an enlightened eye. It is as if, at first, we could only work blindly with our hands; then, after this blind beginning, we learn to wipe our eyes with our hands. Like the psalmist, we 'by Thy commandments have had understanding,'[36] that is, we begin to understand our actions and to discern our affections. The soul is so affected by virtue that, just as God's being is the same as His goodness, so with the holy and upright soul, to be, is to be holy and upright. It is holy in itself, upright towards others, and devoted to God. For by the increase of God's grace, all true love so disposes the upright soul that in none of its thoughts, feelings, or acts, can it possibly be anything but upright. For it has received the imprint of justice deeply and indelibly in its whole being. Hence the Apostle says 'Charity never fails.'[37] At times admittedly we act rashly and unwisely, but that is because charity cannot see except incompletely and through a mirror, in an obscure manner. But for all that, love remains constant.

CHAPTER V

CONSTANT AND INCONSTANT LOVE

THERE are two kinds of love, and of these one is constant and the other inconstant. That love we call constant which is of itself able to possess the soul with a firm hold. Such a possession, however, is only made possible by the help of grace. The other is conceived by varying events, things, and times, and belongs largely to the emotions. The weakness of the flesh often causes it to stumble and fall, causing serious harm and inward pain to the soul. But the soul suffers and submits rather than taking positive action in the exterior evil done. It does not lose charity by its failings; it is charity precisely which makes it grieve and cry out to God: 'Unhappy man that I am, who shall deliver me from the body of this death?'[38] Because of this the apostle says: 'In my mind I keep the law of God, but with my flesh I keep the law of sin. It is not I who do this, but the sin which is in me.'[39] Thus, as Saint John says, in so far as any man is born of God (by which he means the interior man) he does not sin as long as he hates, rather than approves of, the exterior acts which the body of death performs. The seed of his spiritual rebirth, which is from God, protects him within. Even if he is occasionally wounded by the inrush of sin, he does not perish when he falls, for the fundamental charity in him remains unshakenly Godward. And so he rises up immediately, all the readier, all the more able, and with every hope of doing well.

This is how Saint John puts it: 'Whosoever is born of God committeth not sin, for God's seed abideth in him, and he cannot sin because he is born of God.'[40] Consider the full force of these words. He says that that man 'sins not,' for he who is born of God does rather suffer than perform the sinful act. And he adds, moreover, that such a man 'cannot sin'—that is, he cannot persevere in sin as long as he tries to subject his flesh to that law of God which his soul already obeys, even though the flesh may seem to obey the law of sin when temptation and sin rush in. Peter did not lose charity when he sinned, for he sinned rather against truth than against charity. He lied when he said that he did not belong to the One to Whom he did in fact belong, heart and soul.[41] The truth of charity washed away the lie with his tears. Likewise David did not lose charity when he sinned—rather his charity was stunned by the violence of his temptation. Charity was not destroyed; rather did it sleep, and it awoke at the sound of the prophet's reproach, breaking out straightway in that burning confession, 'Lord, I have sinned.' Immediately came the answer, 'The Lord has taken away thy sin. Thou shalt not die.'[42]

Another thing in praise of charity is this. Love is in faith and hope. Charity is in itself, and for itself. Faith and hope can be without charity, but it is impossible for charity not to have faith and hope. Faith asserts the existence of the loved one. Hope promises that we shall possess him. He loves therefore, who loves in faith and hope (in so far as one who as yet can only be believed in and hoped for can be loved). But charity already has and holds the One we believe in and hope for, and already embraces Him. The love of faith and hope desires to see God because it loves Him. But charity loves Him because it already sees Him. Charity, indeed, is the eye by which God is seen. The soul, like the body, has five senses, but whereas the body is joined to the soul by means of its senses, with life as mediator, the soul has five senses wherewith it may be joined to God, with charity as mediator.

This is the reason why Saint Paul says: 'Be not conformed to this world, but be reformed in the newness of your mind, that you may prove what is the good, acceptable, and perfect will of God.'[43] He is showing us how we grow old by means of the body's senses, and become conformed to this world. But by the soul's senses we are made new in the knowledge of God, and in newness of life according to God's will and pleasure. There are, as we have said, five bodily senses, and by means of these the soul gives sense-life to the body. They are touch, taste, smell, hearing and sight. Now the five spiritual senses by means of which charity gives life to the soul, are family love, social love, natural love, spiritual love and the love of God.

CHAPTER VI

THE FIVE SENSES OF LOVE

THE love of near relatives is compared to the sense of touch, for this disposition is inherent in all men and we think of it as common and somehow tangible. It wells up in everyone in the most natural way, and there is no way of stopping it. The sense of touch is wholly corporeal, and it comes about by the contact of any two bodies. Contact will engender touch in any body which is alive. Whatever you do, your body can never be without touch. Likewise your soul can never be without the love which is analogous to the sense of touch. For this reason the love of near relatives does not receive much commendation in holy scripture. In fact, our Lord says: 'Unless a man hate father and mother, he cannot be My disciple,'[44] so that this love may not become excessive.

Social love is compared to the sense of taste. This is brotherly love, the love of the holy catholic church, of which it is written: 'Behold how good and merry a thing it is for brothers to live in unity.'[45] As life is given to the body by means of taste, likewise, by means of this love the Lord sends 'blessing and life for ever and ever.' Taste is admittedly a corporeal function, but its purpose is to bring about the savouring of food within the body, which savouring is for the soul's appreciation. So we may say that this sense is mainly a bodily thing, but quite evidently it also belongs in some measure to the soul. This is equally true of social love, which comes as the result of people living together and of sharing the same profession, or studies, or such like things. It provides a common bond, and grows through mutual help and exchange. It would seem to belong to the soul considered in its relationship with the body (being based on physical cohabitation and common material interests), but it is in a large part spiritual. For just as flavour is in tasting, so does brotherly love yield that love which is said to be 'like perfume on the head, flowing down to the beard, even unto Aaron's beard and to the skirts of his clothing . . . like the dew of Hermon falling on Mount Zion.'[46]

To the sense of smell we can compare natural love, by which we mean that love which causes us to love every man in virtue of our sharing in the same nature, and to ask for nothing in return. It comes from the hidden recesses of our nature, and invading the soul, will not admit anything human to be alien to it, or unkindly.[47] The sense of smell would appear to belong more to soul than body, for in order to smell something, all that is needed on the body's part is a slight intake of breath through the nose. And albeit the smell comes in via the body, it is the soul, not the body, which is thereby affected. Natural love then belongs more to the spirit than to the soul which vivifies the body, for it considers only the human connaturality of the loved one, and has no respect for consanguinity, society, or any other kind of obligation.

Spiritual love we compare to the sense of hearing. By spiritual love we understand the love of our enemies. Hearing, instead of producing its effect within the body, works after an exterior fashion. That is to say, it knocks on the ear and calls on the soul to come out and hear. Likewise the love of our enemies is not stirred in our hearts by any power of nature, nor by any spontaneous affection, but by obedience alone, which hearing signifies. That is why this love is called spiritual, for it brings us to the likeness of the Son of God and confers on us the dignity of sons of God. As the Lord says: 'Do good to those who hate you, that you may be sons of your Father Who is in heaven.'[48]

Divine love is compared to sight, for sight is the highest sense, and divine love is the highest of all the affections. Although it is the eye which sees, sight is in some sense predicated of the other senses, as when we say 'taste and see,' or 'touch and see.' In the same way, it is because of divine love that we may speak of other affections being loves, if they are good. It is clearer than the day that no one is to be loved unless it be for God's sake. A thing is only lovable because of the reason *why* it is loved. Wherefore we read: 'From Whom all paternity is named, in heaven and on earth.'[49] Sight is a strong and pure power of the soul, and the love of God is powerful because it does great things; pure because, as Saint Augustine says in his *Confessions* and elsewhere, nothing impure enters into it. God will not deign to be loved along with anything which is not loved for His sake.

The power of seeing is located in the highest part of the body, and because of this it has all the other instruments of sense beneath it. Those which belong rather to the soul are nearer to it than those which belong more to the body. The least of the senses, and the lowest, is touch, which is most proper to the hand although it is common to the whole body. The mind, which is the head of the soul, must be the seat of the love of God, so that from this position it may illumine, govern, and guard all the loves below itself, giving them of its own warmth and light. The more spiritual loves will be nearer to it than the more carnal ones, when we have learned to love God with all our heart and soul and strength, and when we really love our neighbour as ourselves.

Sight, as we have said, being placed in the worthiest part of the body, has some influence over those powers of the soul which are more exclusively concerned with the body, but it tries to imitate the powers of mind and memory, in so far as it may, traversing the width of the sky or great tracts of country in a single moment. Likewise the enlightened love of God, when it has made its dwelling in a Christian soul, causes it to have some likeness to divine power. For when the soul finds that all its things are God's, and that all things work together for good[50]—(Paul, Peter, life and death, all things whatever being God's) then it finds all created things little and inadequate and insignificant when it compares them with God.

CHAPTER VII

LOVE AND REASON

CHARITY, as we have seen, is the soul's natural light, and was created by the Author of nature for seeing God. There are two eyes to this spiritual vision, forever straining to see the Light which is God, and their names are love and reason. When one of them tries to see without the other it has little success, but when they work together they can achieve great things. Then they are that single eye of which the spouse in the Canticle speaks: 'Thou hast wounded my heart, O my beloved, with one of thine eyes.'[51]

Each eye has a hard task, since reason cannot see God except in what He is not, while love is not content to rest except in what He is. What, indeed, can the reason grasp, however hard it may try, of which it dare say 'This is my God'? It can discover what He is, only by inferring from what it knows Him not to be. Reason has its own fixed routes and straight ways by which it progresses. Love, however, advances more by its failures, and understands more by means of its ignorance. Reason appears to advance from what He is not, to what He is. Love leaves behind what God is not, and rejoices to lose itself in what He is. Love came from God and naturally yearns towards its origin. Reason is careful and wise, but love has the greater blessedness. And when I say that these two help each other, I mean that reason instructs love, and love enlightens reason. Reason merges into the affectivity of love, and love consents to be limited by reason. Then it is that they can achieve great things. But if you ask me what these great things are,

I can only say that this is learned by experience, and that it is meaningless to speak of it to the unexperienced. As it says in the book of Wisdom, 'Into his joy the stranger shall not pry.'[52]

And now the soul, which has so far been tenderly nursed on the sweetness and delight of love, and only occasionally buffeted by the Father's fond correction, this soul, I say, is severed from its cleaving to the world by the swordstroke of a love as strong as death. Love of the world is killed, just as the body is killed by death, and like Enoch it is 'found no more in the world.'[53] In this dying, the bodily senses lose their power, and the soul is thereby made more perfect, quickened and strengthened in all its doings. Now courage and wisdom attend its path, and it perseveres in the way, going on where before it had hardly dared to direct the feet of its good assent, hindered as it was by ignorance, doubt and fear. 'The strength of the upright is the way of the Lord.'[54] The soul makes itself dead to the doings and feelings of the world. As Paul the Apostle says: 'The world is crucified to me, and I to the world.'[55] For when each of these ignores the other, each being bound up in its own interests, neither of them will care to approach the other, nor even have the power to do so. And yet, although Paul's citizenship was of heaven, he did not refuse to come down to earth when it was necessary for men. Because of this he groaned: 'I desire to depart and to be with Christ— a lot by far the better.'[56] How much better it is to be with Christ! For our Lord said: 'Behold I am with you all days, even unto the consummation of the world.'[57] Paul's greatest security is the companionship of Christ. To be with Christ, either in this life by means of contemplation, or in heaven with the possession of eternal bliss, is Paul's greatest joy. The love of God draws him up, and the love of his neighbour bears him down, like a weight hanging from his neck. And therefore he goes on to say: 'Yet to stay on in the flesh is necessary for your sake.'[58]

By means of the love which is charity, the soul cleaves inseparably to God, forming all its judgements by the light of His countenance, and ordering its actions according to the holy will of God which it learns inwardly. It loves to gaze upon God's face and to read there, as in a book, the laws by which life must be governed. It reads and understands; its faith is enlightened, its hope strengthened and its charity enkindled. For now the Spirit of wisdom teaches the holy soul what it must do and by what means it must do it. The Spirit of fortitude provides strength wherewith to accomplish the task, and the Spirit of counsel arranges all things for the work in hand. When the soul is free to cleave to God, it is made like God by loving devotion and union of will. When it is forced to leave the law of God's countenance and ordered to return to men and to human things, it brings grace to them in virtue of the glorious brightness it bears in body and soul, word and deed. It produces such reverence in men that they obey its will unquestioningly. And when it comes, like Moses, from the hidden sanctuary showing a face horned and terrible,[59] it does so only in order to reprove the vices of those who sin, and because the justice and severity of God's judgements make this necessary. But severity appears as charity, and anger is seen as the chastisement of love, when those who are reproved recognize that correction is made only where it is due, and according to the unalterable law of Truth.

The wheels which appeared to Ezekiel, 'having the breath of life,' were always running onward to fulfil God's will.[60] They did not turn back to pursue their own desires. Likewise the holy souls of whom we speak, if made superiors, acquit themselves of their office with all solicitude, and are like fathers to their sons. But if they are made subject to others, then they obey with humility and are like sons to their fathers. If they are obliged to live with others, they do so with charity. If they live in community, they make themselves the servants of all. They are lovingly inclined towards everyone, and live in peaceful agreement about all that is good. They come together with joy, and go out of their way to show charity towards one another. To those who are below them in any way, they show a tender affection in their deeds. On their elders they bestow love to the point of subjection. To those above them their obedience goes as far as slavery. They do not seek their own interests, but those of the brethren. Whenever possible they make the common good their own, in spite of detriment to themselves. For they have received that pledge which is the Holy Spirit's gift, and they know that bodily service will soon pass into the adoption of those who will be revealed as the sons of God. Therefore they find it easy to bend both body and will to whatsoever thing the greatest of commandments orders.

CHAPTER VIII

THE SCHOOL OF LOVE

LET us now pass on to what the Apostle calls 'fellowship in the Spirit,'[61] for I wish to praise the joyous state of brethren living together in unity. When our Lord said: 'Do not be afraid, little flock, for it has pleased your Father to give you the kingdom,'[62] He was calling down upon it long life and blessing. The praises of this life were first sung by the apostles, who learned it either from our Lord or from the Holy Spirit, with whose grace they had recently been clothed from on high. They established a way of life such that the multitude were of one heart and one soul. They had all things in common and with one accord they would all meet in the temple. Since that time there have always been men to imitate the community of the apostles, having neither house nor resting place other than that house of God which is the house of prayer. They do everything in the name of the Lord. They share the same way of life, they live according to one rule, they possess nothing, not even their own bodies. They go to rest at the same time and rise together. They pray and read together, and sing psalms in unison. It is their firm and fixed resolve to obey their superiors and to be subject to them.

The superiors in their turn watch over their subjects, for whose souls they will one day have to render an account, and in so doing they declare, as Gedaliah did to the people of Israel: 'I will answer to the Chaldeans who come to you: but as for you, gather the vintage, the harvest and the oil, and lay it up in your vessels, and abide in your cities safely.'[63]

This means that they must neglect their own portion of the fruits of the Spirit for their subjects' sake. They must make daily sacrifice of their heart's joy, like Abraham who was asked to sacrifice Isaac, the son of the freewoman, and to cherish Ishmael, the son of the slave. In working for their subjects' salvation, they place all longing for their own perfection after the service due to those in their charge. Preaching to them the perpetual sabbath, they make them strangers to the cares of the world and the anxieties caused by want. Their necessities have been reduced to the minimum and they live on little. Their clothes are coarse, their food is plain, and everything else is determined by the measure set out in the Rule. No one may have more than he is allowed (for if everyone has sufficient there is no need to give him more) and in this way there is enough for all.

Is this not a heavenly paradise rather than an earthly one? But in this paradise only the superiors may eat of the tree of knowledge of good and evil, which is to say that they alone can give the wise decisions which prudence dictates. But if any of the subjects should touch the tree when it is his duty to obey, 'let him die the death.'[64] The brethren are always zealous in keeping silence, but they speak to each other by means of their hearts' affection. Fuel is added to fire through the frequent exhortations of the superiors, but the monks incite each other rather by their mutual example. They strive to excel in paying honour and attention to each other, and follow the Apostle's advice by encouraging each other to charity and good works. They allow no one among their number to be a recluse, lest Solomon should say to him: 'Woe to him that is alone!'[65] They reckon him a recluse who admits his unwillingness to have someone share his private affairs, or who upsets the community by introducing strange new ideas. When the matter calls for it, a quiet conversation is allowed on spiritual subjects or bodily needs, but when this is unnecessary, silence seems all the more pleasant. There is so great and unceasing a devotion to the practise of prayer, that every place of prayer is a place where God rules. The psalmody is so reverent, harmonious and fervent, that it seems to be offering to God a melody composed of the very lives and loves of the brethren, and following the rules of charity rather than those of music. And in the common exercise of this charity, in the grace which shines in their faces and in their bodies, the brethren see in each other the presence of the divine goodness; and they embrace it with such love that, like the seraphim, each sets the other on fire in the love of God, and none of them can cease to wish to make the others burn more brightly.

This is charity's own school. Here the study of love is pursued, and here love's disputations held, love's questions answered—but these not with the use of reason alone, since the truths of love must be matter of experience. In this school, those who are tired by their journey lose nothing by taking a rest; neither did the two hundred of David's men who were so spent that they could not cross the brook at Besor.[66] If anyone will sit and 'tarry with the stuff' as these did, he will not perish, nor need he turn back nor go forward, since no law compels him to do so. And here, the baggage (his own and his companions') is the sum of life's necessities which none can dismiss. If anyone sits by the baggage and faithfully guards it, he will hardly be worse off than his companions who go on ahead and win the victory, for he shall have an even share of the spoil.

Now is not this very place where we live the brook Besor where the baggage was guarded? Are not our oppressors a burden to us? Are not the sons we love a perpetual source of anxiety? Yes, there are still battles without and fears within. There is still a long climb ahead of us before we reach the top of God's holy mountain—still a long journey for Jeduthun (which Saint Augustine interprets as 'passing over' in his commentary on the seventy-sixth psalm), still a long way to the house of the God of Jacob.

Surely an old man is entitled to a little consideration when he no longer has the strength to carry his burden. But it is not his years which make him venerable, but his virtues alone. He looks forward to a long rest at the end of his journey, and to the fulness of wisdom which comes as the reward of his labours. Wisdom takes up the journey and carries on to the end. It does not leave charity behind, but rather helps it along. But wisdom is simply tired of carrying charity's load, since it has better things in view, for which it is even now preparing itself so as to enter into the joy of the Lord. Wisdom hates cares of any kind, and seeks to be relieved of all encumbrances, although strength is not lacking wherewith to bear them. The Lord says: 'Thou shalt love the Lord thy God with all thy heart, all thy soul and all thy strength and all thy mind,'[67] in order to encourage the soul to go on and to enter at last into His joy.

CHAPTER IX

THE TASTE FOR HOLY THINGS

THE love which we owe to God is fourfold and entire. In that He says He will be loved 'with all thy heart,' He demands our will. By 'all thy soul' He means all our love. 'With all thy strength' implies the virtue of charity, and 'with all thy mind' means the enjoyment of wisdom. It is the will which first moves the soul towards God, and love carries it onwards. Charity contemplates Him and wisdom enjoys Him. The mind is a worthy place for wisdom, since mind (*mens*) is derived from remembering (*meminit*) or from being on an eminence in the soul (*eminet*). Wisdom, the virtue ascribed to mind, is the highest of all that the soul may possess. Mind is that power of the soul whereby we cleave to God and enjoy Him. This enjoyment is a sort of divine savouring, and for this reason wisdom (*sapientia*) gets its name from tasting (*sapor*). Flavour is in tasting, and no one can worthily tell of the divine savouring unless he has merited to taste God. 'Taste and see how gracious the Lord is,'[68] as it says in the thirty-third psalm. The Apostle says that the word of God is savoured in this way; also the riches of the life to come.[69]

But we must look more deeply into this question of tasting, which gives that savour whereby Wisdom gets its name. First we must say that those who seek after Wisdom must climb up to it by slow degrees, but that this were not enough unless Wisdom herself (as is said in Wisdom's own book[70]) came seeking those who seek for her, coming out to meet them in the streets and showing herself with gladness. Unless Wisdom came to those who seek her, the will of the seeker would not move him, nor would love carry him on in the quest. Neither would charity bring him to contemplation, nor Wisdom, at the last, give him enjoyment. Now having established this, let us go on with our investigation into tasting.

The body of Christ is the whole church, both of the Old and of the New Testament. In the head of this body, that is to say the Old Testament which is the highest and foremost part of the body, there are four senses—sight, hearing, smell and touch. Its eyes are the angels with their piercing contemplation; its ears are the patriarchs with their obedience. Its nostrils are the prophets, who knew things far off. Touch is the sense common to all these. Now before the Mediator came, all these senses were in the head. The rest of the body languished because one sense was missing, namely taste. Without this sense the body could not live, nor the other senses have their full power. For of what use is food to the body if taste is lacking? You can, if you wish, apply food all over the body without any effect; you can pour it into the ears, push it up the nose or anywhere else you like, without doing the least bit of good. But when you taste food, the tasting is followed by a sweet savour which the soul feels within itself. The other senses cannot feel it; only taste distinguishes it, and makes a judgement on it. Then all the senses can, as it were, grow fat on it. Taste, moreover, is located in the throat, which is the border region of both head and body, connecting the two. It symbolizes the truth that Christ in His fleshly condition is made a little less than the angels, and the patriarchs and prophets, Moses, Elijah and the rest. By showing patience and humility He made Himself even less than He had become by reason of the Incarnation. Making

Himself more humble, He cast down God's enemies, and taught His disciples to turn the other cheek.

Christ, coming after the prophets and patriarchs as the borderline between law and grace, between head and body— Christ by the mystery of His humanity, His passion and resurrection, brought out the flavour of whatever in law and prophets, psalms and hymns of the Old Testament, was useful and necessary for the body. Acting as mouth to the body He brought out the flavour of these things— that is to say, Christ the man brought out their meaning (which He Himself was) and this He conveyed into the body by the interior savour of His divinity. 'Christ the wisdom of God is made wisdom to us.'[71]

This living Christ gave life and health to the body, and the body thus made perfect was a joy to Him, and to the angels. A joy, too, for the patriarchs and the prophets who had seen and foretold His coming. As He Himself said, 'Abraham your father rejoiced to see My day; he saw and was amazed.'[72] We, for our part, enlivened and strengthened in that same body by His coming, may say with Saint John, that we have seen, heard, and touched the Word of Life.[73] At the end of every prayer we may say 'through Jesus Christ our Lord,' because we direct all prayer and sacrifice to God through Him, as through our Mediator; and because whatever we hope for from the Father we ask to be poured into the body through that mouth which is Christ. Christ is the wisdom and the sweet savour wherewith we are nourished.

This is the sense of taste which the Spirit of understanding has made for us in Christ; that is, the understanding of God's scriptures and mysteries which Christ opened unto His apostles after His resurrection. When we begin not only to understand, but in some way also to touch with our hands and to feel the inner sense of the scriptures, and the power of God's mysteries and sacraments, then Wisdom begins to offer her riches. This touching and feeling is produced by the inner senses when these are well practised in the art of reading the soul's secrets and the hidden action of God's grace. To those whom she judges worthy, Wisdom teaches all things by means of her anointing. Our powers once softened thereby, the seal of God's goodness brings them into order and conformity. If any of them be stiff or crude, it is broken down and pressed into shape. This done, the joy of God and the princely Spirit of wisdom give strength in such measure that the soul may sing gaily to God: 'The light of Thy countenance, O Lord, is signed upon us: Thou hast given gladness in my heart.'[74] This is eternal life, as our Lord said . . . 'that they may know Thee the one true God, and Jesus Christ Whom Thou didst send.'[75] O blessed knowledge in which eternal life is to be found! This life comes of tasting, for to taste is to understand. Saint Paul, having tasted and savoured the riches of Christ, prays that we may understand with all the saints what is their length, their breadth, their height and their depth, even as he has done.[76] Let us, then, try to penetrate more deeply into the sense of this wisdom of which he speaks.

CHAPTER X

CHRIST OUR MEDIATOR

IN God are power, wisdom, charity and truth (or eternity, which is the same as truth, for nothing is true unless it be changeless). In return for these four things, we owe God fear and love—fear of His power which can punish us, and of His wisdom which nothing can hide, and love of His truth and His charity. Our fear must be true fear, not undermined by indifference and complacency, nor supplanted by presumption on God's mercy. Our love must be true love, without lukewarmness on the one hand, or scruple and mistrust on the other. What can we owe to Charity, if not charity? The truth of charity and the charity of truth will do away with all our lack of confidence in the love of God and in the constancy of His truth and unfailing eternity. Saint Paul asks that we may understand with all the saints what is the length, the height, the breadth and the depth of the mystery of Christ.[77] The height is God's power, the depth His wisdom, the breadth His love, the length His eternity and truth. These are the four dimensions of the Cross of Christ.

Saint Paul prays that the Spirit of wisdom may be bestowed on us in these words: '... I cease not to give thanks for you and remember you in my prayers, asking that God may give you the Spirit of wisdom and revelation, in the knowledge of Him.'[78] God grants this prayer by giving us to know and savour Him through revelation, and by giving Himself as a savour in us. Our eyes are enlightened that we may see the good and understand its goodness—for to this end is the hope of our calling, the 'riches of His eternal glory among the saints.'[79]

In all these things, goodness and kindness appear, enlightening and calling us. And in order that we may follow the one Who calls us, strength is also bestowed. Through our experience of the Spirit of wisdom, the transcending greatness of His truth is revealed to us. We discern and judge all things through the taste of divine contemplation, when that sense of taste, which is the heart, is restored to health. In Christ, the Author of all good, we first taste conversion to God, then the forgiveness of our sins, and later, instead of tasting anger (whose sons we were) the increase of manifold graces delights us. All this comes to us through Jesus Christ our Lord. He is our Mediator and our Wisdom. His foolishness is more wise than men.

The goodness of God was abundantly offered to all men, but none of them was able to receive it, for none of them knew how to receive it. Nor could they teach anyone else how it might be had. None could rise up to the place where God's benefits were being given, in order to bring them down; therefore there was need of a mediator between us and God, through whom we might come close to God, and God's goodness could come down to us. So the Trinity took counsel together, as is said in the thirty-second psalm— 'may Thy ancient counsel be made true.'[80] The Lord saw that all was in confusion and disturbance among men; nothing was in its proper place, nothing went well. He saw that man had gone so far into the land of unlikeness, that he could not of himself return from it, nor could he know how to return. The angels had already presumed on their likeness to God, and they had said: 'I shall put my throne in the north, and I shall be like the Most High.'[81] Man wished to be like God since he had been persuaded that men would be as gods. All men tried to emulate the Son of God,

and to be, as it were, His friends and equals, but in this
they failed. And He, when He saw them perishing through
their disordered yearning after that image in which they
had been made, went to their rescue. 'Only the wretched,'
He said, 'have no one to envy them. Therefore it is only
just that I should go to them. I shall show them Myself,
innocent, despised, a man of sorrows and acquainted with
grief, so that they may strive to copy My humble state and
so find the way to glory. Let them learn of Me, for I am
meek and humble of heart, and they shall find rest to their
souls.'[82]

CHAPTER XI

THE MANNER OF OUR REDEMPTION

THE Son of God prepared Himself, as it were, and came to save whomsoever He could. This He did through humility since man had perished through pride, drawing back from God only to be caught and bound by the devil. Christ became Mediator between God and man by becoming man Himself, as was once prophesied . . . 'There shall come forth a rod out of Jesse, and a flower shall rise up out of his root. And the Spirit of the Lord shall rest upon him—the Spirit of wisdom and of understanding, the Spirit of counsel and fortitude, the Spirit of knowledge and of godliness. And he shall be filled with the Spirit of the fear of the Lord.'[83] Understand by this that our great champion, entering the lists of the world, is anointed with the oil of the Holy Spirit. He is the athlete rejoicing to run the course of man's salvation. See how the prophet, in setting out the gifts of the Holy Spirit, begins with the higher ones and comes down to the lower, by which he means to imply that the Mediator is coming down to us. But we, by the same graces of the Holy Spirit, and by means of the Mediator's action, must begin at the bottom, that is to say with the spirit of fear, when we seek to return to the heights. Christ's fear of His Father was a due and filial fear, through which He gave glory to the Father in all things. As He Himself said: 'My food is to do the will of My Father Who is in heaven.'[84] And in the psalms we read: 'Let my heart rejoice that it may fear Thy name.'[85] Through this fear He seemed to abase and humiliate and forget Himself, so that He could return to His Father, having repaired that creation which, through Him, the Father had originally made.

Our Mediator had fear of His Father, as if of some higher being, but He also had mercy, as on lower beings—that is, upon those He came to reconcile with the Father. He knew the Father and the measure of fear He must show Him. He knew mankind and the measure of mercy that was needed there. But in order to carry out His work of mediation, He required the faith of men. God from above had given Him His good will, but unhappy mankind, grovelling in the earth, had given Him nothing. The nature and function of mediation made it necessary that Christ should require something of man, as He had required something of God. He could make no more reasonable exaction than to ask the faith of men, for already they could see that He was mercifully disposed towards them, and therefore it was not hard for them to entrust themselves to His love. With their trust they also put their hope (since they could hardly entrust themselves to someone in whom they could not hope), and to this they added fear, without which they could have no real hope that the Mediator would never abandon them. Having received such a pledge from mankind, the Mediator at last returned to His Father. He went up to the mountain alone and prayed with a sweat of blood and in agony, asking that His Father might glorify Him so that He might glorify His Father.[86] 'Behold,' He said, 'what love I show to Thee and what love I show to man ! Behold, what pledges I have from him and from Thee ! Even now, My mediation is bringing about his salvation. A strong enemy once captured and bound him, but here is someone stronger to break the bonds. Send down Thy power, then, from above and I will snatch mankind from the strength of the enemy. Let Me, Who am innocent, die for those who are guilty. Let goodness achieve more than malice has done, and may the sufferings of the innocent do more than could be done by punishing the disobedient.'

'I have both glorified,' said the Father, 'and I will glorify Thee again.'[87] Now it is time for the gift of counsel to come to the Mediator's aid, and the Son of God hides the power of His divinity and shows only the weakness of His humanity. For if the prince of this world had understood what was happening, he would never have crucified the King of Heaven. The goodness of Christ's life had stirred up the envy of the wicked. By the weakness of His humanity He gave His enemies a hope of victory over Him; and His miracles, which were performed in order to deepen our trust in Him as Mediator, only helped to increase their envy. And so the old deceiver was himself deceived, making Him undergo a most cruel death and inflicting the punishment of sin on the One Who was sinless. The just man was unjustly killed for justice's sake, but He got from His enemy a new kind of justice, precisely by means of the death He underwent. Being in no way obliged to submit to death, since He was without sin, He gave the merits of His death to sinful man. He was innocent, and He obtained pardon for man's sin by being punished. The Son of God took His body and blood into His hands and said 'Eat and drink, and draw your life from this source.' Offering Himself to His Father, He said: 'Behold the price of My blood, and if Thou seekest a price for man's sins, see here is My blood which will wash them away. Father and Lord, Thou hast given what was good, and the earth of My body has produced its fruit. Now justness shall go before Thee and Thou wilt place Thy feet in the path of man's salvation. Thou hast decreed a right judgement upon man, justly saving him who justly should have perished.'

CHAPTER XII

THE PHILOSOPHY OF LOVE

WITH God's wisdom as mediator, man is filled with the fruit of Christ's act, and he is not only reconciled with God, but also made wise. He eats the body of the Lord and drinks His blood. He savours this bread of angels, bread of wisdom and heavenly manna. As he eats, he is transformed into the nature of his food. To eat Christ's body is to become Christ's body, and to be made a temple of the Holy Spirit. When this temple is embellished with all requisite virtue and dedicated as we have outlined above, it can receive no further titles and no other occupant but the God Who created it.

A holy soul no longer cares for material, earthly and corruptible things, since it has left the place of burdens behind it. Sometimes it uses these things in passing, but it is disinclined to enjoy them as before. If anything goes ill the soul is not perturbed, and if anything goes particularly well it leaves no effect. The soul savours whatever comes along. A lover cannot but savour those things which come from the tasting of Christ. Anything to do with the body, be it good or evil, remains outside. It cannot touch that part which is within. Wherefore the apostle said, when he lay chained in misery, 'I will send Timothy to you, that you may know how it is with me.'[88] That is to say, how it is with me in regard to the external garment of the flesh, the outer man, which things do not touch me inwardly.

This is the wisdom which the apostle 'speaks among the

perfect,'[89] and of which we also speak who have heard but not seen—as we might speak of a city which we have not ourselves had sight of, but about which we have heard much said. And if we had actually seen it, we would be able to say more than we do, describing it more fully. This wisdom, of which it is said 'Wisdom overcomes malice,'[90] is as different from that so-called wisdom which the apostle calls the 'wisdom of the princes of this world,'[91] as white is from black, and light from darkness. Wisdom, as we have already seen, takes its name from savouring (*sapor-sapientia*). Malice, for its part, is the savour of evil. The wisdom of this world's princes, savouring evil, lacking nothing of craftiness and purposefulness in the carrying out of its designs, is wholly contrary to heavenly wisdom. This is the malice which true wisdom hates. The savour of goodness is in the good, and the savour of evil is in the bad. Prudence is at hand for seeking the one: and for the other, as we have said, craftiness is not lacking.

But between these two, namely prudence and craftiness, wisdom is a sort of mean, like the colour between white and black, which is as equidistant from white as it is from black. The wisdom which lies between the two opposites is that which Saint Paul calls 'the wisdom of this world'[92]: not, mark you, of the princes of this world, nor yet of God. It acts in respect of what is good, and is dispensed by means of prudence. It belongs almost wholly to knowledge, so that one may know how to discern with prudence and judge between the useful and the harmful, the good and the bad, however much this knowledge may be at variance with an existing mode of life.

Whereas knowledge puffs us up, charity builds us up. So it is necessary to have more than mere knowledge which leads to curiosity, vanity and self-ostentation. Reason, unaided by love, can lead us only to pride.

CHAPTER XIII

THE EXCELLENCE OF TRUE WISDOM

THIS our philosophy is divided into two sciences—that of things human and the other of things divine. But it is more at home in the human sphere, for when it tries to raise itself up to higher things, it falls all the more heavily. As the psalmist says, 'Thou hast lifted me up and cast me down.'[93] By means of our own efforts, our faculties will carry us a certain part of the way towards God. Reason may know only as much about God as it contains of God in itself. God created us with the necessary faculties for knowing Him, and thus He reveals Himself to us. Starting from the things which we see, we lift ourselves up for a sight of God's invisible things, His eternal power and divinity. From our own moral science we can raise ourselves up to a sort of metaphysics or natural theology, so that, as Saint Paul says,[94] we are inexcusable if we decline to go on from our natural knowledge to the true theology, when God has equipped us with the ability to do so. If we refuse to seek the knowledge of God we are like those who, knowing God, refuse to glorify Him and to render Him thanks. We should be calling ourselves wise when, in fact, we were fools. And if, by our own fault, we were to lose the deeper knowledge of God, neither would we have any profit of our natural knowledge of Him, for we would probably be putting 'the glory of the incorruptible God into the likeness of bird, beast and reptile.'[95] For this reason we are not allowed to make even our moral science an end in itself.

We must go on to find God, else He will abandon us to the desires of our own hearts and allow us to do those things we should not. Wisdom, however, always overcomes malice. Living as it does near to God, it has the knowledge wherewith to go on ever further and never to fail. It will achieve its end and dispose all things pleasantly, acting wisely in respect of divine things, cautiously among the works of nature, and prudently in all question of conduct.

So a wise soul, as we have said, puts off the old man to put on the new, cleansed from all unnatural dispositions and savouring only God. Orientated now in all things towards God, it sees all creatures in the same way that their Creator sees them, ordering and disposing all things in the light and power of wisdom. Acting thus, considering creatures in their true light, its judgements come from the Creator Who gave the soul its birth and life. It lives according to its original nature.

God's wisdom, in the words of Wisdom itself, is the 'purity of eternal light and the flawless mirror of God's majesty.'[96] It is an outpouring of God's radiance, an outbreathing of His power. Bearing within itself both the mirror and the pure light by which to see, the soul, when it shows itself among creatures, expresses to them an image of God's goodness and righteousness. The power of God is present within; His brightness and His charity breathe outwardly, as Solomon says: 'A man's wisdom shines in his face,'[97] and 'The eyes of a wise man are in his head.'[98] The eyes shine forth with that wisdom which is in the mind. The multitude of the wise means the well-being of the whole world. How well, indeed, it would be for mankind if wise men were always respected by fools! Plato says that all would be well if only wise men reigned—or if all those who reigned were philosophers. But in the same way

that wise men wisely avoid ruling fools, so do fools foolishly
refuse to submit to the rule of the wise. And so confusion
reigns; wise men hide themselves away, while the in-
experienced lord it like the princes who 'rise up early to
eat, and woe to their country!'[99] But to return to our
subject . . .

A soul which has been enlightened by the Spirit of
wisdom pleases all men and by all men is loved. It loves
righteousness and hates evil doing. It is anointed with that
oil with which Christ was anointed. Even its enemies
fear and do it reverence. Even though hardened wickedness
may dissuade any ill-disposed person from imitating such
a soul, none can deny the reality of the goodness which is
seen there. The wise have a way of speaking to one another
by means of their mutual love, and this they communicate
to each other by means of a glance, as the angels might—
a language which is special to God's chosen people and
strange to the stranger. Just as holiness of life and the
transfiguration of the inner man become visible in them,
and it is evident that their contemplation is a true foretaste
of the beatific enjoyment of God, so are their bodies also
transfigured in our sight. Living together as one in God,
and enjoying God in themselves, they are no more subject
to the contradictions of the flesh, for all flesh has become
for them an instrument of good works. Even if they are
shaken by its weakness, they are thereby only made stronger,
as was Saint Paul. They are conscious of a new sense, and
of a present grace. They have a temperate ear and a simple
eye. Sometimes when rapt in prayer they catch some un-
known fragrance, and without physically tasting, they are
conscious of a new sweetness. These brethren find that the
least touch carries such an incitement to charity that their
monastery becomes a very paradise of spiritual delight.

Their transfigured faces and bodies, their holy life and behaviour, their mutual service and devotion, so bind each brother to his brothers that their heart and soul cannot but be one. The future glory, which will be perfect in the life to come, stands revealed in them already.

CHAPTER XIV

THE BEATIFIC VISION

Now all living things are flooded with the brightness of the sun, and each one casts its light upon the others. As we see each other to be living, without seeing the life by which we live, likewise in the life of beatitude, God will be seen by each in all and by all in each one of the blessed, without the Godhead being seen by the bodily eye. Rather, the glorified body will show forth the presence of God by its manifest grace. This shows the value of the sacraments in this life. We can understand hardly anything except concrete and physical things while we are passing through this world like shadows, and so God binds us to Him by means of the sacraments which we can perceive with our senses. (The word 'religion' may be derived from *religare*, meaning 'to bind,' and we are bound in this way so that we may not wander from God.)

When a soul, which has been taught by means of the sacraments, is able to leave the means of sense behind it, and to rise up from physical to spiritual things, and from spiritual things to the Maker of everything, both physical and spiritual—then that soul is really leaving behind it the baggage of which we have previously spoken. Leaving the body with all its cares and hindrances, it forgets everything except God. It takes no notice of anything but Him, as if it were indeed quite alone with Him. 'My love is mine and I am his' we read in the Canticle.[100] And in one of the psalms . . . 'What have I in heaven but Thee? And having Thee, I delight in naught upon earth. My flesh and my heart fail, but God is my portion for ever.'[101] Death is only death for the unfaithful soul. For God's true lovers, what is it but Passover? By the death of the body the soul dies completely to the world, to live utterly in God. It goes straight to the place of God's wonderful tabernacle. It enters even into the house of God. Man's natural bent, as we said in the beginning, carries him to his proper end. The body returns to the earth from which it was taken, and from whence it will be raised up again and glorified, and the spirit returns to God Who gave it.[102]

But after all the bonds have been broken and all obstacles have been overcome, then is our passing-over to God brought about, in perfect bliss and everlasting delight. Then does the soul cleave perfectly to God, or rather the truly holy soul is joined to God even while on this earth, so that it becomes one of those of whom it is said: 'I have said that you are gods, and all of you are the sons of the Most High.'[103] This is the goal of those who make Jerusalem the beginning of their joy,[104] whom the unction of the Holy Spirit instructs in everything, who in their hearts go up from virtue to virtue until the God of Gods is seen in Zion.[105] He is the Beatitude of the blessed, the Joy of the joyful, the one and only Good, the highest Perfection. From the time when the soul's good resolve is made, that is from the beginning of the ascent, until the summit is gained, 'wisdom reaches from end to end, mightily.'[106] Wisdom watches over the climber's strength lest he grow weary on the way up; Wisdom 'orders all things sweetly,'[107] whether it be adversity or prosperity, disposing all things for the soul's good until it leads it back at last to the source of its origin, and hides it in the secret of God's countenance. It must be remembered, however, that the stages of love are not like the rungs of a ladder. The soul does not leave the lesser loves behind it as it moves onward to the more perfect love. All the degrees of love work together as one, and for this reason another soul's experience of the scale of love may well follow an order which differs from the one I have described.

NOTES

[1] *Summa Theologica*, II. IIae, 24, 12.
[2] William of Saint Thierry, *Meditations*, translated by a religious of C.S.M.V., page 68, London, Mowbray, 1954.
[3] Genesis iii. 19.
[4] Ecclesiastes xii. 7.
[5] Psalm xxxii. 12; cxliii. 15.
[6] A reference to the *Ars Amatoria* and the *Remedium Amoris* of P. Ovidius Naso. William's refutation of Ovid in this work won it the mediaeval title of *Anti-Nasonem*.
[7] Psalm xlviii. 13.
[8] Genesis vi. 3.
[9] Psalm xxi. 15.
[10] Job xxviii. 28 (according to LXX).
[11] Ezekiel xxiii. 20.
[12] 2 Corinthians v. 13.
[13] Exodus xxxii. 32.
[14] Romans ix. 3.
[15] Acts xxvi. 24.
[16] Psalm lxvii. 28.
[17] Virgil, *Eclogue* 3, 36.
[18] 1 St. Peter i. 22.
[19] 1 St. John ii. 16.
[20] Psalm cxviii. 20.
[21] Romans vi. 19.
[22] Psalm lxii. 5–6.
[23] Ephesians iv. 23.
[24] Job xxxvi. 32.
[25] Canticles v. 1.
[26] 1 Corinthians xi. 29.
[27] Psalm lxxx. 16–17.
[28] Hebrews vi. 4.
[29] Hebrews vi. 7.
[30] Hebrews vi. 9.
[31] 1 St. John iv. 16.
[32] 1 Corinthians xii. 31–xiii. 13.
[33] St. John xv. 15.
[34] Exodus xx. 13.
[35] Cf. Psalm xviii. 5.
[36] Psalm cxviii. 104.
[37] 1 Corinthians xiii. 8.
[38] Romans vii. 24.
[39] Romans vii. 25.
[40] 1 St. John iii. 9.
[41] Cf. St. Mark xiv. 71; St. Matthew xxvi. 69–75.

[42] 2 Kings xii. 13.
[43] Romans xii. 2.
[44] St. Luke xiv. 26.
[45] Psalm cxxxii. 1.
[46] Psalm cxxxii. 2-3.
[47] A reminiscence of Terence's *Homo sum: humani nil a me alienum puto.*
[48] St. Matthew v. 44.
[49] Ephesians iii. 15.
[50] Romans viii. 28.
[51] Canticles iv. 9.
[52] Proverbs xiv. 10.
[53] Genesis v. 24.
[54] Proverbs x. 29.
[55] Galatians vi. 14.
[56] Philippians i. 23.
[57] St. Matthew xxviii. 20.
[58] Philippians i. 24.
[59] Exodus xxxiv. 29.
[60] Ezekiel i. 21; x. 17.
[61] Philippians ii. 1.
[62] St. Luke xii. 32.
[63] Jeremiah xl. 10.
[64] Genesis ii. 17.
[65] Ecclesiastes iv. 10.
[66] 1 Kings xxx. 9. Cf. *William of Saint Thierry*, Meditation XI, page 78, 'I will sit beside the road.' The same image of sitting by the road, and the same train of thought (approaching age, the question of resigning the abbatial charge) throw some light on this passage.
[67] Deuteronomy vi. 5; St. Matthew xxii. 17; St. Mark xii. 30.
[68] Psalm xxxiii. 9.
[69] Hebrews vi. 5.
[70] Wisdom vi. 17.
[71] 1 Corinthians i. 30.
[72] St. John viii. 56.
[73] 1 St. John i. 1.
[74] Psalm iv. 6.
[75] St. John xvii. 3.
[76] Ephesians iii. 18.
[77] Ibid.
[78] Ephesians i. 16.
[79] Ephesians i. 18.
[80] Psalm xxxii. 11 (according to LXX).
[81] Isaiah xiv. 13-14.
[82] St. Matthew xi. 29.
[83] Isaiah xi. 1-3.
[84] St. John iv. 34.
[85] Psalm lxxxv. 11.
[86] St. John xvii. 1.
[87] St. John xii. 28.
[88] 1 Corinthians iv. 17; Philippians ii. 23.

[89] 1 Corinthians ii. 6.
[90] Cf. Ecclesiastes ii. 13; Wisdom vii. 30.
[91] 1 Corinthians ii. 6.
[92] Ibid.
[93] Psalm ci. 11.
[94] Romans i. 20.
[95] Romans i. 23.
[96] Wisdom vii. 26.
[97] Ecclesiastes viii. 1.
[98] Ecclesiastes ii. 14.
[99] Ecclesiastes x. 16.
[100] Canticles ii. 16.
[101] Psalm lxxii. 25.
[102] Ecclesiastes xii. 7.
[103] Psalm lxxxi. 6.
[104] Psalm cxxxvi. 6.
[105] Psalm lxxxiii. 6, 8.
[106] Wisdom viii. 1.
[107] Ibid.